Poems 3/3

Michael Boy works as a writer and conceptual artist. He explores the feelings and peculiarities of special people and tries to capture moments through poetry. An approach and a confrontation.

These poems are dedicated to
Birgit, Max and Leo.

Bibliografische Information der
Deutschen Nationalbibliothek: Die
Deutsche Nationalbibliothek
verzeichnet diese Publikation in der
Deutschen Nationalbibliografie;
detaillierte bibliografische Daten sind
im Internet über dnb.dnb.de abrufbar.

Herstellung und Verlag:
BoD – Books on Demand,
Norderstedt

ISBN: 9783753472010

96 crazy short poems from the main volume "Poems".

Incomprehensible poems by and about special people. In search of encounters, self-discovery and self-help as a mixture of words. An affair of the heart.

Part 3

In the previous two parts, you may
have noticed that all thoughts are
repetitive. So it is also with my other
work, everything repeats itself, repeats
itself almost without end. Just like the
heartbeat. Not exciting, but necessary.
And at some point there is an end. But
until the end we should be alive.

1. Prison

You are confined to trauma prisons
with very limited life.

2. Love

For love,
I forget myself,
question and think.

3. Petition

And we pray to be in the prison of
love,
in the dark history
and again in the prison of dreams.

4. Morning

In the good morning
I remember hope
and forget a good day,
it will be a good day.

5. Reborn

The thought is reborn again and again
and dies again and again.

6. Fear

Fear has impressed you,
a good day is not over.

7. Do not worry
Spring comes to you with me,
whether you are afraid or not.

8. Cross
The two crosses stood in the
mountains
and in me,
carrying one or more crosses,
lost,
hope and crosses.

9. Celebration
We cling to the cross forever,
we give false meanings again.

10. Heaven
When you finally find the gap
and suddenly discover the cross,
begin to curse
and decide.

11. Scratch
Heal wounds of the heart,
properly care for the wounds,
leave nothing in the heart,
poisons or garbage.

12. Unfortunately
Unfortunately,
suffering does not always have a great
purpose,
but it always makes sense.

13. Trust

Please
draw a solid picture with confidence
in your idea.

14. Solidification

When the waves hit me,
I noticed the fire inside me.

15. Sound

A resounding absolute silence hits you
for a moment
and disappears at the first thought of
success.

16. Discouraged
It turns discouragement into a sense of
achievement,
becomes stronger,
wins,
kills,
and finally becomes human.

17. Excitement
Excitement is not excited,
it does not come from anywhere,
it attacks spontaneously
when everything becomes impossible.

18. Candle
Stand up
straight and think of the incredible
calmness
of the candle.

19. Apple
I found the apple,
but the core is a little rotten.

20. Vomit
Friendly vomit smells sour
and destroys my love of wholeness
and understanding.

21. Dandruff
Damp shoulders slightly weakened
the benefits of the game.

22.   Brake

They slow me down with their
superiority,
and I always dream of great things,
and I show you.

23.   Up

When the door opened
and a great king entered,
he was stupid
and stumbled.

24.   Friendly

Become kind again,
accept the world
and rule the world.

In between once find rest, then start
running again and get out of breath.
Being hungry, getting drunk and loving
a lot. Helping others and being happy
in the process.

25. Core
The great difference at the core shows everyone
that there is no difference at all.

26. Say
If you have good phrases or proverbs,
I suggest you sit down
and fly away.

27. Balanced
I sat balanced on the floor
and laughed and died again,
when will you come back?

28. Frost

Please give me the task of being very
mature
and very rough,
losing the beginning
and finding the beginning.

29. Finally

The load goes deep into the earth
and the earth is waiting for you.

30. Sound

The sound is drenched,
loud,
thinks
and says something wise at the end.

31. Love

Remember the love here,
the love of one and the other,
the caring love
and the love of heaven.

32. Darkness

After looking at the plan
and thinking about the day,
the proposals go through the world.

33. Construct

Now,
they have overcome the construct
and captured the good inventions of
life.

34. Game
Invent old games,
feel safe
and communicate with each other.

35. Rain
The raindrop sticks to the glass,
the thoughts stick together with the
living drop
and meet you.

36. Illusion
The illusion of consciousness restricts
my good work
and I breathe.

37. Adjustment

Sounds come from the sounds of
subtle sounds,
the situation narrows,
the morning sun heats up.

38. Reason

A very good reason to live
is to know better
and not to be caught by you or others.

39. Nose

Concentrating on the nose
helps to reach the goal
and die.

40. Observing
The smell on your fingers
opens a new world
and it begins.

41. Without
Especially the word without has great
content
and takes us to the beginning of the
innocent world
and turns around.

42. Useful
It can be used with good intentions
and cannot be lost until the end.

43. Finally

Parts take us to the infinite,
let's check the opinions,
we gladly accept them.

44. Condition

The good condition of the broken
stamps makes us think,
because performance is considered
and then allowed.

45. Sun

The sun innocently passes
into a sunburn.

46. Flourish
The old man blossoms briefly,
looks cheerful,
gets on the last train home,
everything seems fine.

47. Sad
The fish already stinks
and hunger is filled with impatience for
us.

48. Old
Excited,
everyone is running blindly,
breathing fast
and getting old quickly.

Are you okay? Are you missing something for happiness? When will the end come? Do you still have some time?

49. Leg-hard
Right now you have to be strong
and suffer so you can go to heaven
and finally be happy.

50. In the beginning
In the beginning,
the train was lost,
no one heard the sound,
it was not so quiet and first.

51. Unreasonable
All the accused have forgotten
and are unreasonable friends.

52. Travel

Travel long distances
and come to the thoughts of others,
break,
share and run away.

53. Meaning

The sentence reveals a great secret
and remains unknown.

54. Hand

Squeeze the enemy's hand without
strength
and give up life,
and good luck flies to,
manage everything well.

55. Glass

Shards of glass stuck in memory,
no one expected the end now.

56. Food

Throw away food
and become an epicure,
more pleasure and enjoyment.

57. Release

Go to church out of boredom
and think about the final redemption
with determined thoughts.

58. Again

Again and again
the good righteous
seem to be disgusting and unfair.

59. Alien

Not at home in the garden,
hoping to explain it to the aliens
and stealthily hiding the secret.

60. Punctual

Wear the right shirt at the right time
and be on time for the funeral.

61. Dreamy

Dreamily fly through the air,
breathe in other people's smells
and become a better-looking dreamer.

62. Heroes

Since I received a medal,
I can call myself a man.

63. High

The clouds in the sky seem to fly high,
remember the past,
you are a sticker
and laugh.

64. Arbitrary

The driver could not resist,
all the responsibility fell on others,
and even love was a word.

65. Fast

The bird on the windowsill
chirps the morning song too fast.

66. Out

How far from being,
being big,
playing with life,
becoming more
and more and doing well.

67. Responsibility
I hold you responsible,
it's none of my business
how you are.

68. Worm
The worm has found a hole in your
mind,
has found a home here
and will stay with you
until the end of your life.

69. Heart
With an empty heart I meet my heart,
with an empty heart I meet your heart,
with an empty heart I meet a being.

70. Prison
Life in a dream
cage is very limited.

71. Love
Forget yourself in the thirst for love,
think carefully and ask.

72. Inquiries
We pray
and pray with stories to be back in the
prison of dreams,
to be in the prison of love.

73. Morning
Good morning returns hope,
a good day will make you die,
it will be a good day.

74. Born again
To be born again and again,
to be dead again and again.

75. Fear
Fear has touched you,
the good days are not over yet.

76. Without fear
Be fearful or fearless,
spring will come for you
and for me.

77. Crosses
Two crosses stood on a mountain
and in me,
they carried more than one cross
and lost hopes or crosses.

78. Festival
We always hold on to crosses,
they also give the wrong meaning.

79. Emptiness
When you find emptiness
and unexpectedly find crosses,
you start cursing
and will be decisive.

80. Hardened
The wave beats me
and I notice the feast inside me,
protected by the mutes.

81. Sound
The sounding absolute silence hit you
and disappeared with the first thought
of success.

Slowly it comes to an end. But probably no reader will have started from the beginning. Probably not you either. And that's just as well. You don't always start from the beginning. You just jump into the unknown and you get going.

82. Discouraged
Turn sadness into a feeling of success
and be strong,
conquer and kill
and finally become a human being.

83. Excited
Excited is not excited
and does not come from anywhere,
has to do with intelligence
and spontaneous attacks.

84. Candle
Just get up
and think clearly
and by candlelight,
think of incredible happiness
and just rest.

85. Apple
I found an apple,
but the apple was rotten.

86. Vomit
Friendly drunken vomit smells sour
and dissipates my love for honesty
and understanding.

87. Dandruff
The scales on the shoulders
easily weaken the superiority
in the game.

88. Drakes
You brake me with your superiority,
and I always dream of great
possessions,
and I will show you.

89. Wise
When the door opened
and the great sage entered,
he stumbled stupidly.

90. Kind
Be kind,
accept
and rule the world again.

91. Core
The great difference in the core
shows everyone that there is no
difference,
we plant and die.

92. Suggestion
A good suggestion
and a good saying invite you
to sit down
and fly away.

93. Balanced
Sit down well on the ground,
laugh and lose again,
how right is it
when you return?

94. Frost
Be very mature
and very rude,
lost the beginning
and set ourselves the task of finding
the beginning.

95. Last
The burden pulls you
deeper and deeper into the earth,
the earth is waiting for you.

96. Sound
Permeated by sounds,
by soft and loud sounds,
think
and finally say something wise.

End. A happy ending. Hopefully.